W9-BYF-521

Here's To You, Mom!

by
SCHULZ

HarperCollins*Publishers*

Wish You
Were Here

MOM Wish You Were Here

WHEN I WAS LITTLE AND I DIDN'T FEEL WELL, MOM WAS ALWAYS THERE...

I NEVER SHOULD HAVE LEFT HOME..HOW CAN I TELL MOM NOW THAT MY STOMACH HURTS?

Mother
Knows Best

It's The Thought That Counts

Have a happy Mother's Day.
love, Spike

POSTAGE DUE <u>17¢</u>

Produced by Jennifer Barry Design, Sausalito, CA
Creative consultation by Kristen Schilo
First published 1998 by HarperCollins*Publishers* Inc.
10 East 53rd Street, New York, NY 10022
http://www.harpercollins.com

ISBN 0-06-757452-1

Printed in Hong Kong

1 3 5 7 9 10 8 6 4 2